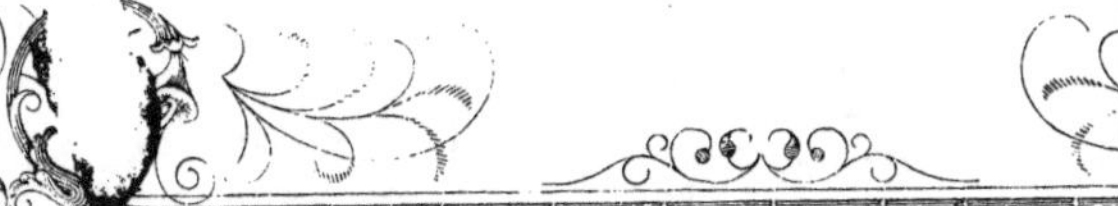

THE PILGRIMS AND THEIR PRINCIPLES:

A SERMON

BEFORE THE

NEW ENGLAND SOCIETY OF PITTSBURGH,

On the Evening of December 22d, 1850,

IN THE THIRD PRESBYTERIAN CHURCH.

BY D. H. RIDDLE, PASTOR.

PUBLISHED BY REQUEST.

PITTSBURGH:
PRINTED BY W. S. HAVEN, CORNER OF MARKET AND SECOND STREETS.
1851.

THE PILGRIMS AND THEIR PRINCIPLES:

A SERMON

BEFORE THE

NEW ENGLAND SOCIETY OF PITTSBURGH,

On the Evening of December 22d, 1850,

IN THE THIRD PRESBYTERIAN CHURCH.

BY D. H. RIDDLE, PASTOR.

PUBLISHED BY REQUEST.

PITTSBURGH:
PRINTED BY W. S. HAVEN, CORNER OF MARKET AND SECOND STREETS.
1851.

PITTSBURGH, Dec. 25th, 1850.

REV. DAVID H. RIDDLE, D. D.

Dear Sir:—The undersigned, members of different Committees of the New England Society of Pittsburgh, and representing the wishes of the Society, and in its behalf tender you most cordial thanks for your excellent and eloquent Discourse to our Association, at your Church, on the 22d inst. And we respectfully request that you will furnish us a copy for publication.

We regret that, in the excitement of our Jubilee on the succeeding evening, this request, with our thanks to you, was inadvertently omitted.

Very respectfully yours,

GEORGE F. GILLMORE,
L. R. LIVINGSTON,
JAMES RICHARDSON,
MOSES F. EATON,
LUKE LOOMIS.

PITTSBURGH, Dec. 28th, 1850.

MESSRS. GILLMORE, EATON, LOOMIS, &c.

Gentlemen:—The Discourse you request for publication, was prepared under many disadvantages; yet, if its publication will subserve the cause of truth and righteousness, it is at your disposal.

Yours very respectfully,

D. H. RIDDLE.

SERMON.

"Your fathers, where are they?"—ZECH. 1:5.

ON the 22d of December, 1620, (N. S.) corresponding with the 11th, (O. S.) the inmates of the Mayflower, one hundred and one in number, landed on *Plymouth Rock*, after a long and tempestuous voyage of ninety-eight days across the ocean, and after having solemnly united themselves together in covenant, "as a civil body politic," to find a home, and plant a church, and rear civil institutions, on gospel foundations, in this new world of the West. Few in number, indeed, but strong in faith, and gifted with almost prophetic intuition of the future, they thus and there began to "lay the foundations of many generations," and build, as if for immortality. Doubtless, as they left the land of their birth and early years, and "the place of their fathers' sepulchres," like our first parents as they left their Eden home,

"Some natural tears they dropt, but wiped them soon;
The world was all before them where to choose
Their place of rest, and Providence their guide."

Committing themselves to this guidance, and trusting in Him, in the dreariest intervening storms,

"Nobly the Mayflower bows
While the dark waves she plows,
On to the West!
Till from the tempest shock,
Proudly she lands her flock,
Where, on old Plymouth's Rock,
Freedom found Rest!"

Memorable epoch in the history of man, and the development of God's purposes towards our race! The traveler, when he reaches the spot where some mighty river takes its humble origin, pauses with unutterable emotion, and traces its after and ever widening progress, till it reaches its estuary. With similar, yea deeper emotion—with sublime awe indeed—we may mark the spot whence streams of deepening and widening moral and religious influences began—influences yet rolling onward, and whose ultimate expansion baffles all present calculation. Verily, the little band on this frail bark, compared with the millions left behind, in the beautiful language of inspiration, might be called "an handfull of corn on the top of the mountain." But already "the fruit thereof shakes like Lebanon." Nations have felt its power; all lands have gazed on the spectacle; and the world's destiny, beyond all doubt, has been vitally shaped by the event.

"They little thought how pure a light,
With years, would gather round that day;
How Love would keep their memories bright;
How wide a realm their sons would sway!"

Or, as portrayed in another beautiful figure, "Like grass of the earth," with a self-perpetuating, and self-expanding power, "they of the city have flourished" ever since!—Yes, "like grass of the earth," with a living power, which neither the frosts of winter, nor heats of summer, nor change of climate, nor expansion of territory, can affect, this transplanted seed has been spreading from that spot, North and South, East and West, from frosty Maine and the Green Mountains, to sunny California and to Oregon—from Niagara to the Isthmus—dotting with verdure as rich and beauteous as when it first took root, regions that stretch from one ocean to the other. Already "their line has gone out through all the earth, and there is no speech or language where their voice is not heard." God's eye only can measure the ultimate results of an event which was so small in its beginnings, on the world's ordinary scale of measurement. "This Puritan Saxondom," says Carlyle, "was only despicable, laughable then—nobody can manage to laugh at it now. It is one of the strongest things under the sun at present."

Since the year 1769, when "the Old Colony Club" first observed this anniversary, an honored and honorable custom has sanctioned the celebration of this event, the landing of the Pilgrims, by the sons and daughters of New England, wherever they are scattered over the world. On the same principle that Rome, in her palmiest days, thus honored the rearing of its walls by Romulus; and the Israelites, by God's command, remembered through all their generations, "the night of the Passover;" and many Christians at this period, a mightier event than either, the advent of the Redeemer, "Forefathers' day" is observed in various ways, "wherever two or three are gathered together," who trace their honored lineage back to the early settlers of New England, and their small beginnings, to the rock of Plymouth!

In the arrangements of Providence, this year it falls on the Sabbath. Wisely and appropriately, therefore, you have purposed to add the solemnities of religion and the auxiliaries of the sanctuary, to all the other hallowed and hallowing associations of the occasion. And though I have not a drop of New England blood in my veins; though I am out and out a Scotch Irish Presbyterian, and have never denied my origin; been unwilling or ashamed to own my parentage; born and brought up in the "sunny South;" you have kindly honored me with an invitation to address you at this time. Without any affectation, I may say that I would greatly have preferred that the older person whom you first selected, himself a son of New England, (Rev. Dr. Swift,) had found it convenient to have stood here to-night; as in justice to myself, I ought probably to add, that literally only a few days have been allowed me for preparation. Yet, bound as I am by many tender ties, with the living and the dead of New England, and identified with some of them for the best portion of my ministerial life, I could not refuse, at this invitation, to attempt to supply his place, and improve this occasion.

The time and the place—the day, and the house of God—if no other considerations, will prevent me from spending this hour in mere empty generalities and indiscriminate laudation. Like Elihu of old, I would say, "Let me not, I pray you, accept any man's person; neither let me give flattering titles to any man; for in so doing my Maker would soon take me away." Another course, I am sure, will be a better compliment to your intelligence and conscience, and better comport with my profession, and the circumstances and solemnities that now surround us.

As a guide to our meditations, we shall use the text in the spirit of the prophet's first application of it, to direct your attention to *the distinctive principles of your forefathers, and the best means of honoring them.* And may that God who "hath made of one blood all nations to dwell on the face of the earth," and hath brought the representatives of almost all nations to dwell in unity in this land, give us his presence and blessing to make our meeting redound to our improvement and his glory!

The spirit of the Pilgrims—the principles of the Puritans: the secret of their energy and success, and the lessons which Providence would teach their children and the world by their history!! What themes more befitting the anniversary of Forefathers' day, occurring as now on the Sabbath? God, by the mouth of the prophet, bade the Israelites "look to the rock whence they were hewn, and to the hole of the pit whence they were digged." "Look," says he, "to Abraham your Father, and Sarah that bare you, for I called him alone, and blessed him and increased him." Thus we would say, "your fathers," who and what and where "were they?" and what made them the men whom you, and at last, though slowly, the world now delight to honor?

We say at last and slowly. For within comparatively a short period, much ignorance and prejudice, on these subjects, existed almost everywhere out of New England itself, and even there prevailed to an extent scarcely credible, and not at all creditable. Even since my youthful reading began, great changes have taken place. It was once, and not very long ago, fashionable to caricature the Puritans and their principles, in conversation, romances and sober histories. Even their own children have sometimes thus perverted their pens, and portrayed their sires as Walter Scott did the Covenanters of Scotland. Living authors have stooped to give piquancy to their paragraphs and zest to their romances, by flings at the Puritans, thus stamping "scarlet letters" on themselves, if not on the objects of their aspersions. By many the Pilgrims have been esteemed morose, intolerant, and intensely bigoted—sincere indeed, but ignorant and fanatical; sticklers for trifles; martyrs to logomachies, corresponding with the apostle's delineation of a very different class of persons "doting about questions and strife of words to no profit;" men whose countenances were "never unbent with hilarity or clothed with a smile;" whom restless discontent with society, unhallowed ambition or miserable avarice, drove to these shores, better to prosecute schemes in which they were disappointed at home, and who brought into the wilderness all the usual sourness and asperity of baffled aspirants. "The faith and patience of the saints" have been severely tried by these aspersions, and we might almost fancy "the souls beneath the altar crying out, Oh Lord, how long!" Except among a very select number, the character of Cromwell was utterly misunderstood, even up to the publication of the characteristic work of Carlyle, in which the old Hero is made to speak and act before us in life-like reality. Even the mass of the learned, following blindly the teachings of Hume, were startled to find him anything better than a hypocrite or a fanatic. I well remember, when comparatively a boy, the thrill of astonishment, as well as of admiration, sent through the literary world by Macauley's since celebrated Eulogy on the Puritans, first published in the Edinburgh Review, giving his candid impressions of their character, before he had trodden the slimy purlieus of courtly power, or had his judgment distorted by visions of political preferment or disappointment. I well remember, too, when to my mind "the blue laws of Connecticut," long since proved an impudent fabrication, were as authentic as the books of Moses, as doubtless they are still to many who deem themselves well read and candid men. In many memories, till comparatively a late period, the only incidents in the early history of New England that stood out prominently, were the burning of witches and the persecution of the Quakers, while the memorials of long suffering, patience, and sublime devotion to truth, were either never known, or forgotten with the dreams of childhood! Thanks to the filial piety and affection of her sons, and not least, to anniversary occasions like the present, where the best talents of New England have been invoked and employed, these things are beginning to be better understood, and the mists are rolling away. Thanks, too, to the providence of God, the frail memorials of every day incidents—the records of perils and privations made amidst their endurance, the diaries of the great and good have been preserved to some extent—like Sybilline leaves, more precious as they are diminished! The world could better have spared the records of blood-stained ambition! In these their characters and principles are best written and studied.

These men, the Pilgrims of Plymouth, and all associated with them in the same general enterprise, and imbued with the same spirit, for we wish to be understood as speaking of the whole class—the forefathers of New England, in whatever light they are viewed, were remarkable men; men trained by God for a special mission, and destined, as the world grows older and more candid, and the results of influence are more properly adjusted, to occupy a brightening page in the history and memory of the world! And to specify some particulars—

First, we have always thought that a distinguishing trait of their character and great secret of their power, was, *their intelligent and supreme attachment to the Bible, the written word of God, the only infallible rule of faith and practice.* "They stuck unto God's testimonies." This was emphatically true of these men, as it was of Wicklif, Tyndal, Miles Coverdale, of whom they were the legitimate succession, and of the author of the 119th Psalm, with whose spirit they were so fully imbued. "They stuck unto God's testimonies," both against the antiquated perversions of authority, and the plausible or reproduced novelties of the times; amidst the crowned and coroneted and mitred power of opposition in the old world, and the drearier influences of solitude and desolation in the new. "The word of God that liveth and abideth," like its author, "the same yesterday, to-day and forever," amidst falling thrones and changing dynasties—the sunshine and the storm of this lower sphere—this was the source of their inspiration, the secret of their energy, the mould of their character, the very magic of their might. For the privilege of reading it, and of being governed by its decisions, their fathers had "resisted" even unto bonds and blood, "striving against the sin" of imposing in its stead, human enactments and mere church authority; and for the same privileges and rights, the sons, worthy of such sires, came to this wilderness as Pilgrims, like the woman in the Apocalypse, fleeing to the place which God had provided.

"Jupiter illa piæ secrevit littora genti."

It was from the Bible directly, as containing infallible and ever expansive truth, adapted alike for all ages and all relations, they derived those germinal ideas of rights for which they struggled there so long and manfully, and which God's providence designed should ultimately have such a vaster theatre for expansion here. They "accounted," as they say, "nothing ancient or venerable that would not stand by this rule, and nothing new that would." "That your faith be right and divine," say they further, "the word of God must be the foundation of it, and the authority of the word, the reason of it."

After all, the primary impulse of their struggles, and the reason of their enduring privation and exile, and the untold trials of their new position, was freedom to believe what God had written, and to worship God, as he himself had prescribed. Amidst the deepest gloom of their long "fight of faith," they were animated by the precedents and principles treasured, as they believed, for this very purpose, in the Book of God. Its biographies and histories, predictions and psalms, proverbs and parables, gospels and glorious promises, were to them like household words, from the cradle to the grave. Their ideas of civil rights and attainments in political science, then unexampled by the wisest of other times, and since so highly praised and by some deemed their special glory, were strictly incidental to their main drift and design, growing out of the obvious and necessary application to the present and civil relations of life and society, of principles wrought out in another sphere and for a nobler purpose. These achievements, whence

Locke derived his political philosophy, and to which even Hume ascribes all the true liberty of the British nation, these men considered but secondary. They may have erred, as others have done, (for they were not and never deemed themselves infallible, or to have found full light on all subjects,) in attempting to order the constitution of Church and State too strictly, according to their views of the model, especially of Old Testament teachings. As good Presbyterians, of course, we deem their institutions in the Church too democratic, and as good Republicans, too popular in the State, for any beings but angels, or any government but a Theocracy! Still there can be no question that reverence for the supreme and sole authority of the word of God, was one of their guiding principles, and in a great measnre made them the men they were—"men wondered at," hated and calumniated while they lived, and now, admired and honored by all capable of rising to the apprehension of the true elements of their greatness!

They were men also of *indomitable faith in the invisible and the future*, meaning by this latter term now, not exclusively the future of another world, but the ultimate temporal results of present conduct and influence. This we have always considered one of the essentials of true greatness; the distinguishing trait of a genuine hero; an indispensable qualification in those who are to leave a mark on their age, and shape its after destinies. Faith in the invisible and future, in this sense, springs from familiarity with the word of God, and the abiding habit of reverence for it, as the only infallible source of authority and guide of expectation. From what we have said, therefore, it is not strange, as from what we know it is certain that this was a distinguishing characteristic of the Forefathers of New England. This might indeed be said to be "the spirit of the Pilgrims." The facts of their history, from the beginning of their struggle with arbitrary power, till the establishment of their civil and religious institutions, can be explained on no other principle, granting them to have been men of intelligence, as unquestionably they were, and also "men of like passions with others," affected while in the flesh by surrounding influences and the pressure of visible and present objects. In vain to account for the course chosen by these men, and pursued with such invincible pertinacity of purpose, do we appeal to ambition, though it is a mighty passion, and they have been accused of it; or to avarice, though this has wrought wonders; or the love of pleasure—even slander and malice has not ventured on this plea of explanation. No! no! The men of ambition and covetousness—the lovers of pleasure and votaries of power—were found then, as always, in other ranks, and treading a different path from that of the Pilgrims. They avow this principle over and over again, in the plainest language, and in circumstances where there was no temptation to be insincere. After stating other reasons for their self-expatriation, "Lastly and not least," says Gov. Bradford, "was a great hope and inward zeal they had of laying some good foundation, or at least to make some way thereunto for propagating and advancing the kingdom of Christ into those remote parts of the world; yea, though they should be as but stepping stones unto others, for performing so great a work." Yes, there it is! in their own quaint but expressive language. There is the principle revealed, as it struggled in their bosoms, and has been recorded by their pens just before "the memorable embarkation at Delft Haven."

And if ever men exemplified this principle by their lives, as really as Noah, Abraham and Moses, these men did. The philosophy of Puritanism is "the substantiation of things hoped, and evidence of things not seen." Divine philosophy! "Beyond their perilous path, indeed, hangs the bow of promise, and the Western star of empire," but too dim and distant for any eye but that of faith, to discern, or any heart but that of piety, to appreciate. The timid and time-serving, the mere adventurer, lured by golden visions, as the thousands now pouring into California, or the followers of Cortez and Pizarro, or the volunteers who recently rushed into Mexico; these would have quailed before uncertainties and privations, where only the promises and precedents of God's word, and the claims of conscience, counterbalanced all that was naturally terrifying to the human heart. Yes! they were men of faith, after the pattern of him "who went out, not knowing whither he went."

A few men in successive ages, from Abel down to the present times, have been found able and willing to live by faith in the invisible and future, animated by the hope of distant results, amidst present darkness, and ready to sacrifice present honor, ease and emolument, to be approved of God, and do their generation and the world some service, and to be enshrined in the memories of a grateful posterity, when the mausoleums of the mighty have perished. On such, the destinies of the world have usually hung; by them, chiefly, its onward course has been accomplished, and on them, after all, the best honors and immortality, even of earth, will be bestowed. Your minds will immediately recur to such men as Russell, and Hampden, and Algernon Sydney. During their lives, they are seldom fully appreciated. Their principles are too noble and unusual, to be generally understood. "Their names" are often "cast out as evil," by cotemporaries, and their principles vilified by adverse partizans. "They wander about in sheep-skins and goat-skins, in dens and caves of the earth." Their bodies are not allowed decent burial, or permitted to rest in their graves, by the insatiate malignity of their foes; history, in the hands of their adversaries, blackens their character; and sometimes remote ages only do them tardy justice, and make up by their eulogies, for long cycles of defamation and obloquy.

Such are the heroes of faith; heroes in God's esteem, and to the eye of angels; "of whom the world is not worthy." And such were the Pilgrims—suited to the emergency—qualified to sway aright and decisively the even balanced hinge of Destiny, and put forward, to some purpose, the predestinated progress of human affairs. Without faith in the invisible and the future, their character is inexplicable and their conduct an enigma. With this key of explication, we need not wonder at what they were, or what they accomplished, and are accomplishing still. "To him that believeth, all things are possible."

Even the world, whose creed excludes all that is not visible and palpable and ponderable, is beginning to see and appreciate the glories of faith in these concrete exemplifications. Literature is becoming disabused of its long perpetuated lies. Under the touch of genius, like the bones of the prophet, these long buried giants stand in stalwart majesty before us. In the capital of our country, the pencil of art gives perpetuity on canvass, to the sublime heroism of the Pilgrims; and those who lead "the forlorn hope" in the battle of principle, gather enthusiasm and energy as they gaze on the faces of Brewster, and Bradford, and Miles Standish and his wife Rose, and the rest—the jewels with which the Mayflower was freighted, and New England's early coronet was adorned. Were there no God, and no future and invisible realities—no after rectification of cotemporaneous judgments, and no appeals from the present to posterity, then indeed might the Pilgrims be pronounced fanatics or fools; and so might all that followed them through the furnace, to their future crown and lasting "recompense of reward."

"The peculiarity which has seemed to me," says one who had studied and seemed to understand this principle of their character, "to distinguish these trials from those which the general voice of Literature has concurred to glorify as the trials of heroism; the peculiarity which gives to these, and such as these, the attributes of a truer heroism, is this—

that they had to meet them on an obscure and distant stage, with no numerous audience to look on and applaud, and cast its wreaths on the fainting brow of him whose life was rushing with his blood, and unsustained by a single one of those sterner and more stimulating impulses and aims and sentiments, which carry a soldier to his grave of honor, as to the bridal bed! *Where* were the Pilgrims, while in this furnace of affliction? And who *saw* and took thought of them? They were *alone* in the earth! directly and solely 'in their great Taskmaster's eye!' Had every one of them died the first winter, of lung fever, been starved to death, or crushed by the tomahawk, who was to mourn for them? A few hearts at Leyden would have broken, and that had been all! Unlike the martyr, even, around whose chariot wheels and horses of fire, a congregation might come to sympathize, and be exalted, and blasphemers struck with unwonted admiration—*they were alone in the earth.* Primeval forests, a winter's sun, a winter's sky, circled them about, and excluded every sympathizing human eye. To play the part of heroism, in its high places and its theatre, is perhaps not so very difficult. To do it alone, as seeing Him who is invisible, was the stupendous trial, and 'peculiar glory' of the Pilgrim heroism."

Again: They were men *trained for the posts they occupied, and the work they performed, by the experience of previous trials.* As far as we have studied the book of God's providence, with the explanations of his word, this is the usual school in which he graduates men for greatness—a principle from which he did not depart, even in the case of Him who was chosen for the greatest work the universe was ever called to witness, and the results of which are to fill eternity with praise. "Though he were a Son, yet learned he obedience by the things which he suffered." "The trying of faith worketh patience;" gives root to principle and stability to character. Eminent decision of character, wherever it occurs in the history of time, and especial qualifications for the great emergencies of our world, as far as we have discovered, have invariably been wrought out by this process. Run your minds over the records, and see if it has not been so, from Abraham down to Washington.

Even the ivy, you may have observed, whose very nature it is, to lean on a stabler object, if thrown off entirely from all props, will tower, self-supported, to the skies. The analogy has often been carried out to perfection, in persons of naturally delicate texture of mind, when exposed to a succession or long continuance of desolating tribulations, which have removed the ordinary objects of human confidence.

The youthful trials of Joseph; his separation from his brethren; his servitude in a foreign land, and even his incarceration on the charge of a lying and libidinous woman, constituted the necessary discipline of his future greatness, the dark, but heaven designed steps to his after glory.

Such was the schooling of the Puritans, from their earliest days. In childhood, many of them had seen their parents, for conscience sake, hurried to loathsome prisons, or to be tortured on the rack, "not accepting deliverance," gained only by confession of falsehood or abandonment of principle. Many, born to prospects of affluence, had seen their paternal estates confiscated, and their names and characters held up to contempt by the minions and satellites of power, and the professed successors of the apostles. Their earliest and strongest ideas, as their widowed mothers clasped them to their heart, were of life, as a strife and struggle with "spiritual wickednesses in high places." They were hunted "like partridges on the mountains," from one end of their country to the other, for no crime, but loving the truth, for which their fathers had died, and by which their mothers were sustained and cheered in their desolations. Tired with vexations and hopes deferred, they at last exiled themselves in the Low countries. There they wrought at manual labor, and many, among the rest one who afterwards became the Governor of the Colony, bound themselves apprentices to handicrafts of different kinds, to obtain an honorable living, and liberty of conscience, and to worship God and obey his ordinances. They bore the yoke in their youth, and in manhood bowed themselves to toil, thus to be fitted for the sterner toils and privations which only strong hearts could endure, and from which imagination itself shrinks back appalled. In no other school could they have been so effectually trained for what Providence had in store for them. All the lessons of their youth and manhood, and the well developed "muscles of the mind," were needed to bear up amidst the wintry storms and that heart sickness of baffled expectations, and the horrors of famine and pestilence, which marked the first years of their pilgrimage, "whilst they calmly waited in that defile, lonelier and darker than Thermopylæ, for a morning that might never dawn." Yes! these men were trained, as are all the instruments of the great purposes of Providence, by previous discipline. To explicate aright their patience and noble faith, and strong endurance and manhood, yea, gianthood of character, we must study the story of their antecedent tribulations, for such results fall not out by chance. Heroes start before us, on the tableaux of history, like the Baptist before the wondering inhabitants of Judea; but the philosophic student goes back to the dispensation of "locust and wild honey and camel's hair," the training of the desert, or the lonely cell or the prison, to trace the germs of greatness, and God's process of its development. Had they been dandled on the lap of luxury and ease, or yielded to the seductions of pleasure, or cowered beneath the frowns of power; had they been "clothed in purple and fine linen, and fared sumptuously every day," and not "chosen afflictions with the people of God," as Moses of old, they never would have reached the rock of Plymouth, or planted there the seeds of Empire. Their names, instead of being held in everlasting remembrance, would have rotted with the thousands in every age who prefer "the pleasures of sin for a season," and the gifts of power. But for their trials, we should not be here to-night to commemorate their achievements. They were tried men, who learned truth in the right way, by having it wrought into them. They were made men, as Luther used to say ministers were to be made, by temptation; and "the trying of their faith" has already "been found unto praise and honor and glory;" and no doubt the gold of their character will become brighter and more glorious, with revolving years and coming generations.

Again: Notwithstanding all that has been said or insinuated to the contrary, they were men *of liberal and cheerful piety*. In both these respects, they were in advance of the age in which they lived, the true standard for estimating character and greatness. It would be amusing, if it were not so contemptible, to hear men blaming the Puritans for not acting according to our light, when even pigmies can climb on the back of giants.

In reading again the records of the Pilgrims, in hurried preparation for this discourse, (a field I would gladly have traversed further,) this fact has arrested my special attention, viz: that they were ready and resolved to welcome *new light* from every quarter, and believed that it was yet to come. "If God," says Robinson in his farewell address at Delft Haven, "shall reveal anything to you, be as ready to receive it as ever you were to receive any truth by my ministry; and I am very confident that the Lord has more truth and light to break forth out of his holy word." "He took occasion," says Winslow, speaking of this valedictory, "to bewail the fact that the Reformed Churches would go no further than the instruments of the Reformation, the Lutherans sticking at Luther, and the Calvinists at Calvin; a misery," said he, we are speaking now as historians only, not advocates, "much to be lamented; for though these men were precious and shining lights in their times, yet God hath not revealed his whole will to them; and were they now living, they would be as ready to embrace further light, as that which they had received." We call that liberality! These men were not *hidebound* in their notions, considering all truth stereotyped by past human hands, for all ages; frowning on new investigations, as sins against antiquity; making "men offenders for a word," or a new pronunciation of Shibboleths; subjecting them to pains and penalties for unessential deviations from established formularies; or any unguarded "infringement on the frame-works reared around the Bible by venerable hands in former ages." They expelled the Quakers for their indecency, not their heresy; and the Papists, for their politics, not their religion. They believed in *development*, in the true sense of the term, and expected it "out of God's holy word," where they knew all objective truth had been placed by its author, like the stars in the firmament, immutable in itself, amidst all the improved and ever improving appliances of its investigation and elimination. They did not deem themselves infallible or perfect; prerogatives they attributed to God alone and his holy word, but not to their interpretations of it, a distinction vastly important, and which they were capable of making and maintaining, though it is practically and frequently ignored by many who are "in reputation for much wisdom." They thought that truth, provided it were genuine coin from the mint, lost nothing, and was likely only to gain by earnest discussion, and the mutual and kindly collisions of mind and pen. They deemed it a poor compliment to truth, its Author, or its advocates, that it must be established by power, or shrink from investigation. "Whereunto they had attained, they walked by that rule, and minded" and loved and tried to maintain "that same thing;" but resolved that "if in anything they were otherwise minded," or heterodox, they would also abandon it, when God "revealed it to them." Judged by the light of our age, they may have erred, possibly they did, in the proper application of the principle; but this was one of their principles fully grasped and clearly enounced. This principle, in fact, constituted the very gist of the long continued and terrible controversy of their fathers, occasioned only by the question of vestments and genuflexions, imposed by church authority; a controversy which, in some form, and by some occasion, must continue, and be ever renewed, while there are free minds existing on the one hand, and usurpations of power and the wrong use of authority in matters ecclesiastical, on the other. It will be a sad day for truth and freedom, whatever incidental or lamentable abuses may attend it, when the sons of the Pilgrims, or those who have caught their spirit, anywhere or for any reason or plausible temptation, or unworthy timidity, shall be seduced or scared into an abandonment of this prerogative, and permit a heritage which cost so much, to go by default, or be wasted away by gradual encroachments, which they consciously or unconsciously sanction!

And strange as it may sound in some ears, the piety of these men was cheerful, as well as liberal. We say emphatically, their piety. There is "a laughter of fools, like the crackling of thorns under a pot," to which they made no pretensions, and which would have redounded as little to their honor, as it would have been congruous with their general character. There are some manifestations of hilarity, since fashionable and sanctioned by professors and even dignitaries of the church, which they did not, and probably with a good conscience could not adopt, deeming them unmanly, as unchristian, especially as they were the favorite amusements of their persecutors and oppressors in the old world, and "hating," not without reason, "even the garments spotted with the flesh." Still their piety was cheerful; a serious joy, sublimely glad in God, and in the conscious possession of hopes and heritages, which the frivolous neither knew or could appreciate. The lineaments of Joy, as she descended from heaven to light up their countenances and inspire their melodies, possibly were somewhat soberer and sterner than in halls of sensual festivity, or when she stimulates to "trip the light fantastic toe," amidst the mazes of the dance. But after all, it was the genuine article; "the joy of the Lord, which is the strength of the heart;" a calm and quiet joy, in unison with the wintry snows that surrounded them; light from heaven, tinging the clouds and darkness of their dreary pilgrimage. They understood the scriptural prescription literally—"Is any merry, let him sing psalms!" "When embarking at Delft Haven," says Winslow, the future Governor of the Colony, then twenty-six years old, "when the ship was ready to carry us away, we refreshed ourselves, after tears, with singing of psalms, making joyful melody in our hearts, as well as with our voices, there being many in the congregation expert in music. Indeed, it was the sweetest melody mine ears ever heard." How often, in their long imprisonment in the cramped cabin of the Mayflower, and amidst the wintry waves, did they repeat these songs of joy! Afterwards, the hills of New England, clothed in virgin snow, often echoed them, even from the graves of the early dead!

Call you these men sour and morose? Are Puritanism and Asceticism synonymous, as has been insinuated? Was there not in their composition, a vein of *Allegro*, as well as *Penseroso?* When, a few weeks ago, I stood in the Rotunda at Washington, and gazed on Weir's picture of the Embarkation, with no thought then of this application, I confess I never beheld manly cheerfulness smiling through tears, and rosy joy, blended with sweet sadness, more beautifully embodied, than in Miles Standish, the soldier pilgrim, and his lovely bride, destined alas! to fill the first grave on "Cole's Hill," the pilgrim's burial place, "where," as one says, "the restless waters chafe and melt against its steadfast shore, the unquiet of the world composing itself at the portals of the grave."

Once more: They *were law abiding men, friends of good order, and supporters of the Constitution of their country.* They aimed indeed to place the Constitution on its right basis, and give it its right interpretation against the usurpations and perversions of arbitrary power; and when this could not be done, they left home and native land, pretermitting their rights after a manly struggle, to re-assert and perpetuate them on another, larger and heaven provided theatre. Yes! the Puritans were law abiding men. Why, they cut off Charles' head by provision of Parliament, without allowing their sympathies with suffering chivalry to interfere, or "the higher law" against regicide, to trouble their consciences or palsy their hands when they signed the bill. They dealt with "thorough" going Laud and Strafford, according to statute, when they believed their country was in danger, and compelled his sacred majesty to acquiesce and participate in its execution!

It sounds strangely now in our ears, (I confess it made me feel strangely, on a recent re-perusal,) to hear these men, the victims of oppression, exiles for conscience sake, stript of fortune and defamed in character, by royal tyranny and fraud, using these words in the compact they signed, in the cabin of the Mayflower, before landing: "In the name of God, amen. We whose names are under-written, *the loyal subjects of our dread sovereign Lord, King James I.* by the grace of God, of Great Britain, France and Ireland, Defender of the Faith," &c. Yes! loyal still! And further—"Having undertaken, for the glory of God, and the advancement of the Christian faith, and *the honor of our King and country*, a voyage," &c. Verily, this Loyalty is a thing of life! Impalpable, and with our education, inexplicable, especially when manifested towards an abstraction, or a very little thing, but still a reality, living, operative, tenacious and influential! Would to God it were better understood and exemplified in regard to our country and Constitution! See these men again, when they were under the strongest possible or conceivable temptations to nullify and repudiate the obligations of a compact, mutually acknowledged with the merchant adventurers, men of utterly diverse principles and aims from themselves! See them rising above all pleas of necessity and new discovery of disadvantage, in "the abundance of their poverty," resolving and obligating themselves to pay every shilling contained in the bond, "swearing to their own hurt," as many an honest man may do, and has done, in this queer world of our's, but "changing not," as many, with great claims to conscience, feel themselves justified in doing, to the scandal of their manhood, and to the reproach of their christianity, if they wear that sacred, oft stolen livery!

Oh! if these men were now alive and enjoying the benefits and blessings of our Constitution, a compact mutually acknowledged by the good and great men of our whole country, where, amidst the agitations of this period, would they stand? Would it not be an insult to their memories, to doubt whether they would not be found with the order-loving, covenant-keeping, Constitution-preserving party, at "such a time as this?" Could the ghosts of these men, which seemed to haunt me as I was penning these lines in my solitary study, and even now seem to hover around us, as we portray their principles to their posterity, appear amidst these surges of excitement, to some of their children, what would they say? Like the tremulous and sightless Patriarch, would they not exclaim, "The voice is Jacob's voice, but the hands are the hands of Esau!" Our sons, indeed, but "ah! they've sadly altered!"

Such was the spirit, and such were some of the principles of the Pilgrims, the men whom you delight to honor; from whom you deduce your origin, and who have bequeathed these principles as a sacred heritage to their children. We might turn over other leaves of their history, every one rich in incident and fraught with lessons of instruction and example. If we were curious and so disposed, we might, too, pick out some "dead flies" amidst "the ointment" of their memories. If we taxed our reading and recollections, we might trace some "little follies" in these men, deservedly "in reputation for much wisdom;" and without bearing false witness, probably, or being blamed with malice, we might give some darker colorings to the picture. Such things have been done, and there are some who take special delight and evince peculiar capacity in such business; men who, in a lovely landscape, have eyes only for deformity; in a beautiful portrait can seize upon the slightest defect, seen or surmised; in a glorious character, or class of men, can feed upon infirmities or infelicities, apparently with no taste for excellence or sublimity. "If," as Macauley says, "in any part of any great example, there be anything unsound, these flesh-flies detect it with unerring instinct, and dart upon it with ravenous delight." To such fingers, optics and taste, we prefer to leave the ungracious task. We would rather imitate the conduct, and inherit the blessing of Shem and Japhet, than follow in the dark footsteps and bring upon ourselves the dire curse of Ham, the father of Canaan, the first on record, though the race is not likely soon to become extinct, who gloried to tell his brethren of their common father's nakedness. Instead of this, we would close this imperfect portraiture of singular excellence, having only shades incident to human beings, by repeating a part of the splendid Eulogy, to which allusion has already been made: "The Puritans were men, whose minds derived a peculiar character from the constant contemplation of superior beings and eternal interests. Not content with acknowledging, in general terms, an overruling Providence, they habitually ascribed every event to the will of that great Being, for whose power nothing was too vast; for whose inspection nothing was too minute. To know him, serve him, enjoy him, was, with them, the great end of existence, and hence originated their contempt for terrestrial distinctions. The difference between the greatest and meanest of mankind, vanished when compared with the boundless interval which separated the whole race from Him on whom their own eyes were constantly fixed. They recognized no title to superiority, but his favor. If their names were not found in the registers of heralds, they were written in the book of life. If their steps were not accompanied by a splendid train of menials, legions of angels had charge over them. Their palaces were houses not made with hands; their diadems, crowns of glory which should never fade away. On the rich and eloquent, nobles and priests, they looked down with contempt; for they esteemed themselves rich in a more precious treasure—eloquent in a sublimer language—nobles, by right of earlier creation, and priests, by the imposition of a mightier hand. They had been rescued by the hand of no common deliverer, from the grasp of no common foe; ransomed by the sweat of no vulgar agony, the blood of no earthly sacrifice. The intensity of their feelings, on one subject, made them tranquil on every other. Death had lost its terror, and pleasure, its charms. They went through the world, insensible to fatigue, not to be pierced by any weapon, or withstood by any foe; a brave, wise, honest and useful body." We appeal from Macauley now, to Macauley then, in answering the question, "Who were the Puritans?"

And now, ye sons of New England! children of such sires, do you ask, by what methods can you most effectually honor these men and their principles? We regret that we have detained you so long, that we cannot, without violating too far the proprieties of time and place, dwell, as would otherwise be pleasant and desirable, on this topic. But it is the less necessary, as you have probably anticipated me in most that I have to say.

It will readily occur to you, that it is comparatively easy to admire exhibitions of excellence. It is a grateful, and not difficult thing, to eulogize departed greatness and goodness; to be warmed and thrill at the recital of heroic actions, and to weep over the records of suffering virtue. Ah! if all who admire the characters of history or romance; who sympathize with suffering virtue, portrayed by the hand of Genius, or acted before them on the stage; or who can dissolve in luscious tears over the pages of fictitious heroism, would thereby become great, good, virtuous and heroic, how different our world would be from what it is! The illusion is apt to come over us, that we possess, or are assimilated to the excellence we so unfeignedly admire, or can so eloquently applaud. And yet it is a very different and much more difficult thing, to imitate and exemplify these excellencies in our own character and conduct. Many an one has gone from the theatre, where the mirror was held up to nature, and virtue's self personated by the tragedian, to deeds of darkness and debauchery. Many have risen, in tears, from a novel, to shut their doors in the face of actual suffering, and close their purses and their hearts against pleading poverty. Yea, men have gone from the sanctuary of God, from hearing and applauding the heroism of the apostles, and the sacrifices of the Saviour, to clutch with a sterner grasp these ill-gotten gains, or grind with grimmer heartlessness, the faces of the poor. The Saviour himself speaks of some who built or beautified the tombs of the prophets whom their fathers killed; and who, in their self-deception, declared that if they had lived in those days, they would not have done so. Nevertheless, by their deeds they demonstrated that they were the children of their fathers, and that the same spirit, evidenced in a different way, was still within them.

It is not enough to study, admire and eulogize the character and deeds of the good and great, though this in its place is well. It is not enough to assemble on anniversary occasions like the present, to commemorate events, and listen to the recital of lofty principles and heroic achievements; or to sing the tunes they sung, and drink toasts to their memory, as you propose to do to-morrow night, though all this is proper and praiseworthy. It was a happy conception, worthy of its origin at old Plymouth, and God forbid I should say aught against these means of keeping alive and fresh the memories of the past. But after all, there is "a more excellent way." The true way of honoring the principles of our fathers, is to imitate and exemplify them in the spheres where God has placed us, and to the extent that his providence gives us opportunity!

You can best honor your fathers, and prove yourselves worthy of such parentage, by imitating and exemplifying their sacred reverence for the supreme and sole authority of the word of God in faith and practice; by sticking, as they did, unto God's testimonies; thus steering between antiquated follies and errors, however sanctioned; and pestilent novelties, however plausibly portrayed or pompously paraded, as the spirit of the times and the oracles of right Reason; by making the Bible, as they did, "the light to your feet and lamp to your path," "the man of your counsel," and arbiter of your perplexities, whatever pride, or power, or popularity, or present gain, may plead to the contrary.

The sons of the Pilgrims will best honor their sires and commend their principles, by imitating and exemplifying their indomitable faith in the invisible and future, by whatever present appearances disheartened, or temptations assaulted. They were satisfied with the smile of God, and calmly awaited the judgment of Posterity. Their record was on high, and already, their earthly recompense of reward is exceeding great. No regrets ruffle their placid bosoms now, as no sufferings or privations made them sullen then. "Through faith and patience they now inherit the promises" by which they were once sustained. Go ye, and do likewise, "enduring" even as they, "as seeing Him who is invisible."

Honor, too, your Pilgrim sires, and prove that their blood yet courses undefiled in your veins, by patiently enduring, if need be, the same discipline by which they were schooled for greatness, and qualified to meet the emergencies of their career, and work out sublime problems in the onward course of human progress. Be just men, and tenacious of purpose, when it is right and well advised; and be neither deterred by the frowns of power from doing or suffering what conscience and your reading of God's will, tell you is right; nor swayed or caused to swerve by the whispers or hosannahs of an applauding populace, so as to mount on the turbid waves of a transient leadership or advocacy of wrong. This "mens conscia sibi recti," will carry you calmly through all the privations you have to endure, and will be a brazen wall of defence, better than armaments of power, or treasures of wealth, gotten by disloyalty to truth, amidst all the perils you have to encounter.

Be, once more, as becomes your honored parentage, men of enlightened, liberal, catholic and cheerful piety. Because you believe the truth, you need not be bigots or persecutors. Because "you know your rights, and knowing dare defend them," do not appeal to fire and faggot, or contumely, or caricature, against your adversaries, or bolster up your courage or credit, or approve your rectitude by accidental majorities or unrighteous auxiliaries. We do not exhort or advise you to be latitudinarian, or reckless of your reputation for soundness in the faith, or patrons of every fresh whimsey from the fertile brains of would-be reformers or philanthropists; but still welcome new light, as they did, and be on the side of progress in truth and righteousness, in matters social, civil and ecclesiastical. And try to prove, too, that principle is not moroseness, nor the highest heroism inconsistent with innocent hilarity, singing songs of joy, even as they did, in the house of your pilgrimage, and diffusing around you the radiance of a piety, as attractive as it is uncompromising!

And lastly, be as they were, law-abiding men; true lovers of your country, your whole country, united in one family compact, entered into and solemnly ratified by your fathers and our's, to promote the blessings of union, and perpetuate our institutions to the end of time, and for the benefit of our race! Stand by these United States, and our Constitution, let who will calculate the value of the Union, and the profits of dissolution! Frown upon the first approaches towards the formation of parties, on sectional or geographical lines, let what storms be gathered around you for so doing, from within or without—from foreign foes or domestic traitors! Love your whole country, the loveliest the sun ever shone upon, over all of which your brothers and sisters are scattered, or your sons and daughters may hereafter wander. For so would your fathers do, if they stood where you stand; and such a course, if I have studied their history and principles aright, their spirits will approve, as their example recommends.

"Oh! ye who boast,
In your free veins, the blood of sires like these,
Lose not their lineaments! Should mammon cling
Too close around your hearts, or wealth beget
That bloated luxury, which eats the core
From manly virtue; or the tempting world
Make faint the Christian purpose in your souls,
Turn ye to Plymouth's beach, and on that Rock,
Kneel in their foot-prints, and renew the vow
They breathed to God."

www.ingramcontent.com/pod-product-compliance
Lightning Source LLC
LaVergne TN
LVHW011141110826
845150LV00008B/2460